Piano • Vocal • Guitar

BEST OF THE STAPLE SINGERS

Cover photo: Gems / Redferns

ISBN-13: 978-1-4234-2985-2
ISBN-10: 1-4234-2985-0

HAL•LEONARD®
CORPORATION

7777 W. BLUEMOUND RD. P.O. BOX 13819 MILWAUKEE, WI 53213

Visit Hal Leonard Online at
www.halleonard.com

BE WHAT YOU ARE

Words and Music by HOMER BANKS,
CARL HAMPTON and RAYMOND JACKSON

Medium R&B

Poor man, _ you ought to stop
Just be-cause your neigh-bor's child
Don't try to live as high at as you

tryin' to live a rich man's life.
tends some pri-vate school,
see your boss man do.

Don't go out and buy _ a
you try to send yours, _ but
Just re-mem-ber _ you

Ca-dil-lac if you know _ your mon-ey ain't right. _
know-in' all the time you're real-ly not a-ble to. _
work for him, and he _ don't work for you. _

You'll
If there's

*Recorded a half step higher.

find ____ it's so much ___ eas - i - er ____ liv - in' with - in your means.
Don't try to live like ___ a king on a poor man's pay.
some - thing that you want, ____ and you know you can't af - ford ____

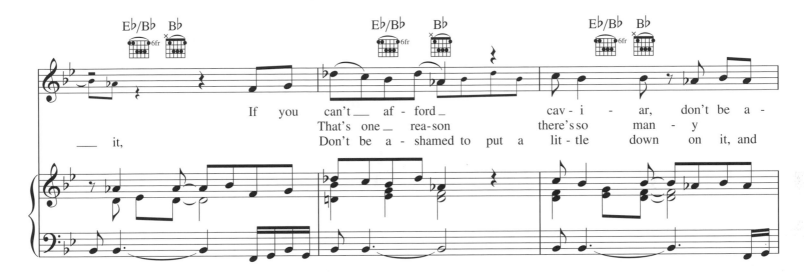

If you can't ___ af - ford ____ cav - i - ar, don't be a -
That's one ___ rea - son there's so man - y
____ it, Don't be a - shamed to put a lit - tle down on it, and

shamed to eat pork and beans, ____ yeah.
peo - ple a - hurt - in' to - day, ___ oh. ___ I'm not tryin' ___ to
tell the la - dy to hold ___ it, yeah. _

tell you how to do it. I'm on - ly say - in', put some thought ___ in - to it.

Be what you are, my friend, ___ and live the life.

Be what you are, ___ my friend, ___ and live ___ the life. ___

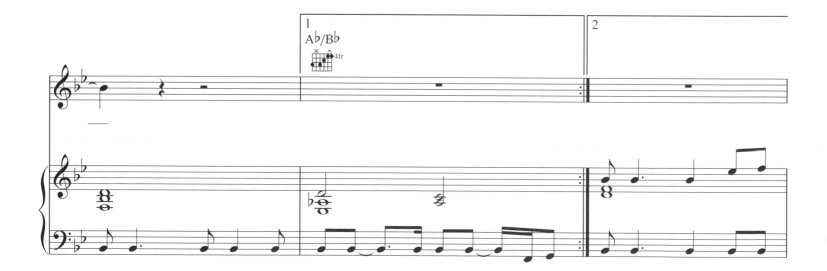

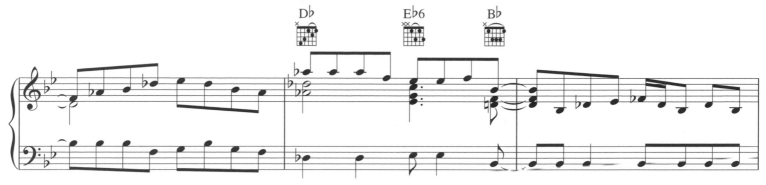

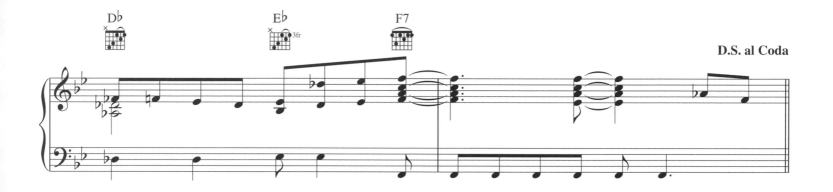

D.S. al Coda

Be what you are, __ my friend, __ and live __ the life. __

Be what you are, my friend, and live the life.

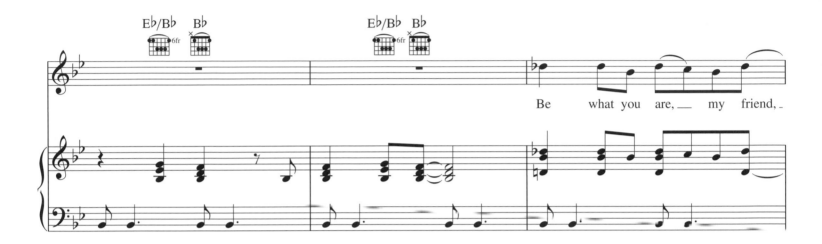

Be what you are, my friend,

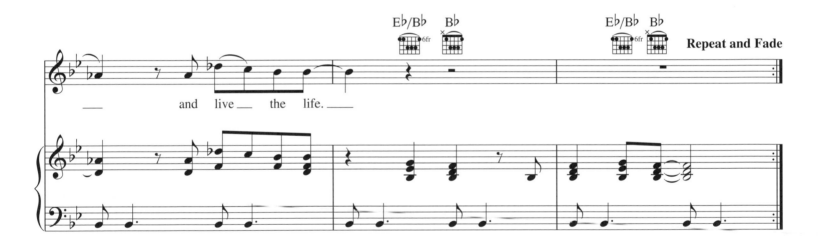

and live the life.

Repeat and Fade

Optional Ending

Be what you are, my friend, and live the life.

CITY IN THE SKY

Words and Music by CHARLES CHALMERS,
SANDRA RHODES and DONNA RHODES

Funky R&B

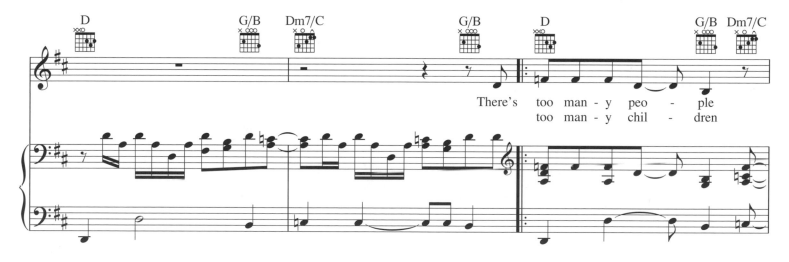

There's   too   man - y   peo - ple
too   man - y   chil - dren

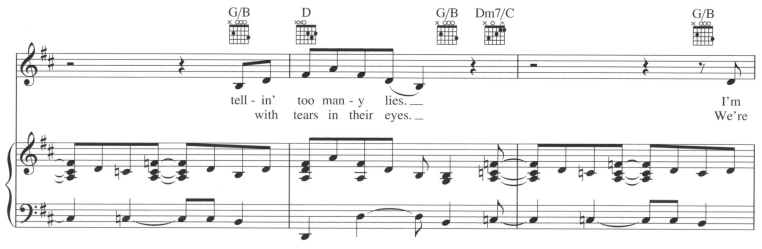

tell - in'   too   man - y   lies. ___
with   tears   in   their   eyes. ___

I'm
We're

gon - na have to build me a cit - y in the sky, ___
gon - na have to build them a cit - y in the sky, ___

where I can fly ___ a - way, yeah. ___
where they can fly ___ a - way, oh. ___

A

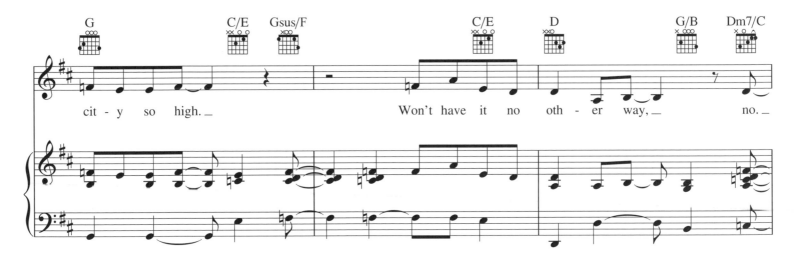

cit - y so high. ___ Won't have it no oth - er way, ___ no. ___

{ I sure ain't gon - na miss the cit - y I leave be - hind. ___
{ They sure ain't gon - na miss the cit - y they leave be - hind. ___

Drag af - ter drag, _ it's blow-in' my mind _ a - way, _ yeah. _
Drag af - ter drag, _ it's blow-in' their minds _ a - way, _ oh. _

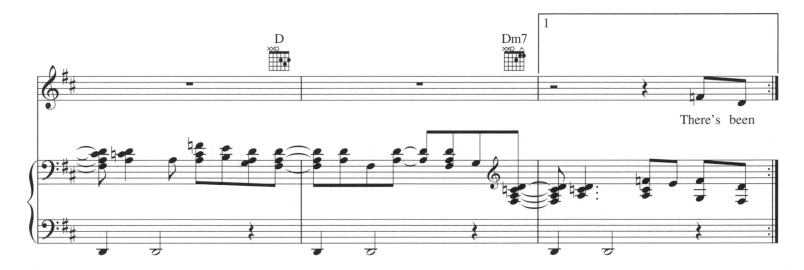

There's been

It's been quite a fine morn - ing, _ it's been

quite a fine _ day. What a feel-in' just know-in'

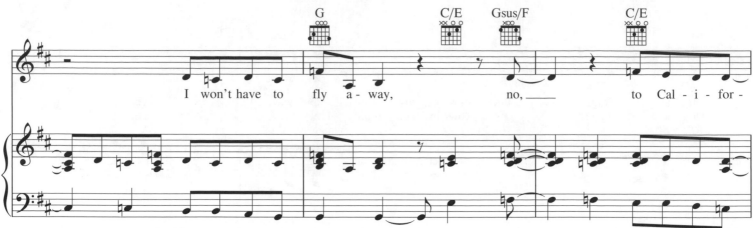

I won't have to fly a - way, no, ___ to Cal - i - for -

- nia, mm, ___ to - mor - row morn - in', ___ no. ___

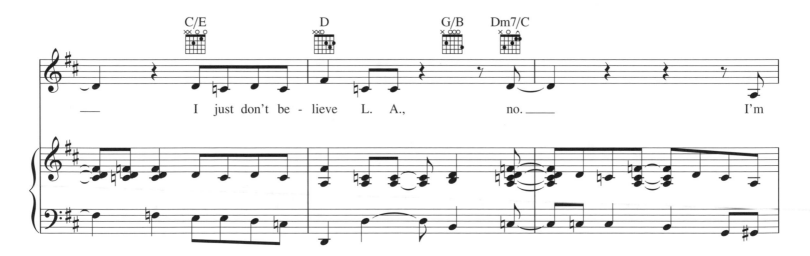

___ I just don't be - lieve L. A., no. ___ I'm

gon - na miss the cit - y, mm, mm, I leave be - hind. ___ Drag af - ter drag, ___ it's

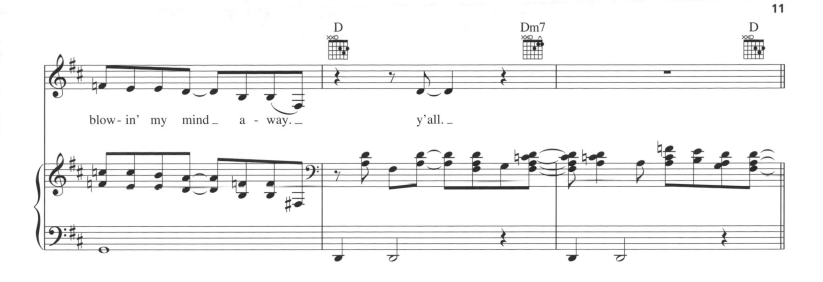

blow-in' my mind_ a-way._ y'all._

Repeat as necessary

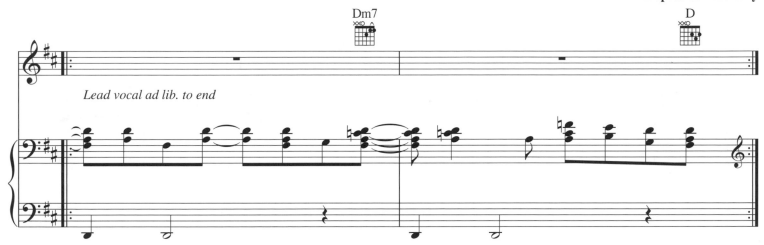

Lead vocal ad lib. to end

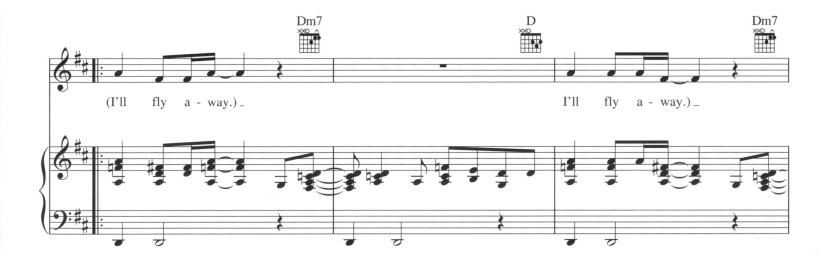

(I'll fly a-way.)_ I'll fly a-way.)_

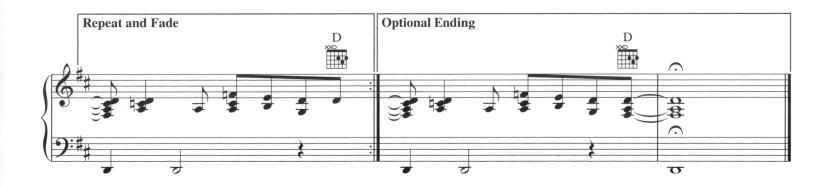

Repeat and Fade

Optional Ending

HEAVY MAKES YOU HAPPY

Words and Music by BOBBY BLOOM
and JEFF BARRY

Well, _____ well. (Sha - na - na - na - boom - boom, yeah.) I've been

tryin' to find what's heav - y that's been mess - in' up my mind. _
By talk - in' to my peo - ple, you know what? It oc - curred to me. _

_____ I _____ think I found _ the an - swer, 'cause it was a -
_____ It's more than just a feel - in',

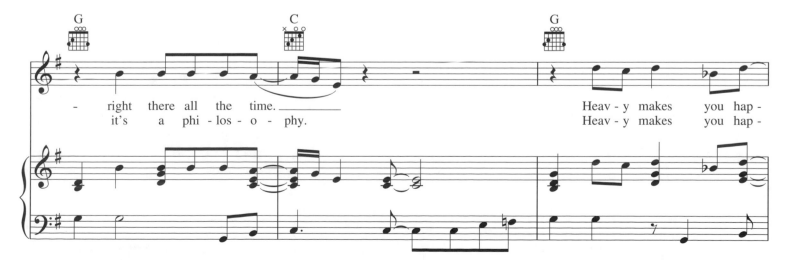

- right there all the time. _____ Heav - y makes you hap -
it's a phi - los - o - phy. Heav - y makes you hap -

- py.   (Yeah.) _____ I just got to say. ___ (Ooh.) _____
- py.   *(ad lib.)* Dry - in' up your drink. __ *(ad lib.)*

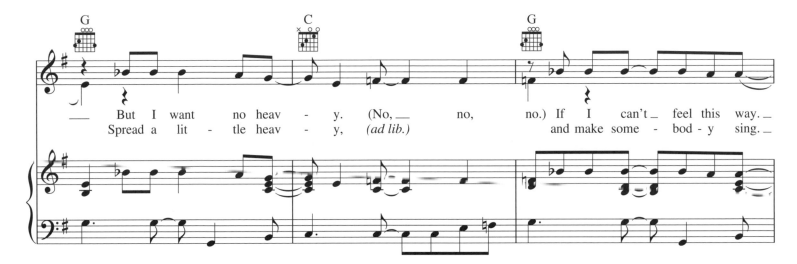

___ But I want no heav - y. (No, __ no, no.) If I can't_ feel this way. __
Spread a lit - tle heav - y, *(ad lib.)* and make some - bod - y sing. __

___ I feel it to me now. (Sha - na - boom - boom, yeah.) ___ Come on, now.

(Sha - na - boom - boom, yeah.) Do it, do it, do it, do it, do it. (Sha - na - boom - boom, yeah.) _
((ad lib.)

Oh. ___ (Sha - na - na - na - boom - boom, yeah.) Oh. ___

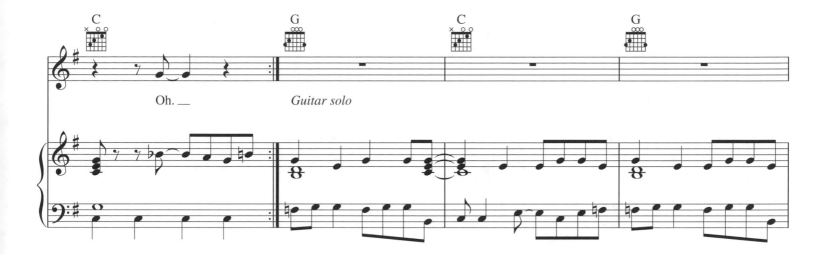

Oh. ___   *Guitar solo*

(Sha - na - boom - boom, yeah.) ___ A lit - tle bit soft - er, now.

(Sha - na - boom - boom, yeah.) Oh, do it eas - y, now. (Sha - na - boom - boom, yeah.) ___

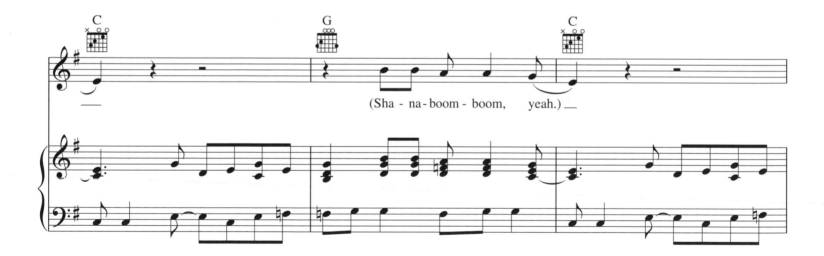

LET'S DO IT AGAIN

Words and Music by
CURTIS MAYFIELD

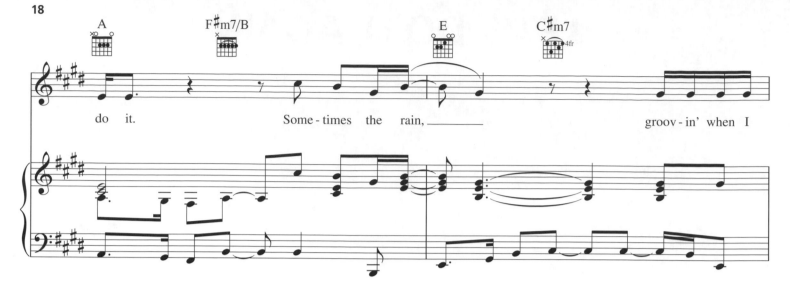

do it.   Some-times the rain,___   groov-in' when I

hear the sound. _   Like you and me, ba - by,___   get-tin' down with the

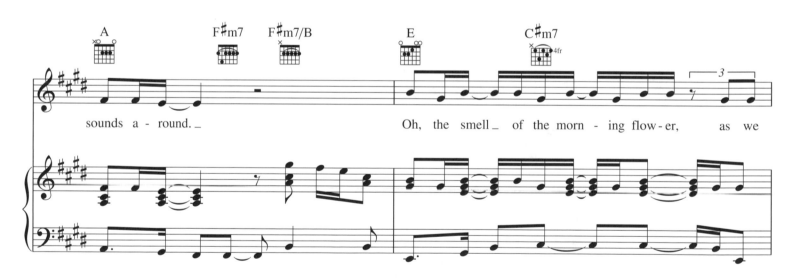

sounds a - round. _   Oh, the smell _ of the morn - ing flow-er,   as we

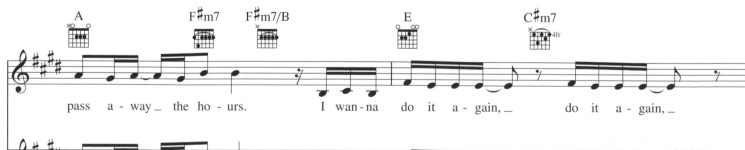

pass a - way _ the ho - urs.   I wan-na do it a - gain, _   do it a - gain, _

do it.　Let's do it in the morn - in',　sweet breeze ___ in the

sum - mer - time. ___　Feel - in' your sweet face　all laid ___ up

next to mine. ___　Sweet love ___ in the mid - night,　good sleep come

morn - in' light. ___　No wor - ry 'bout noth - in',　just get - tin' good,

20

just get-tin' good, just get-tin' good lov - in'.

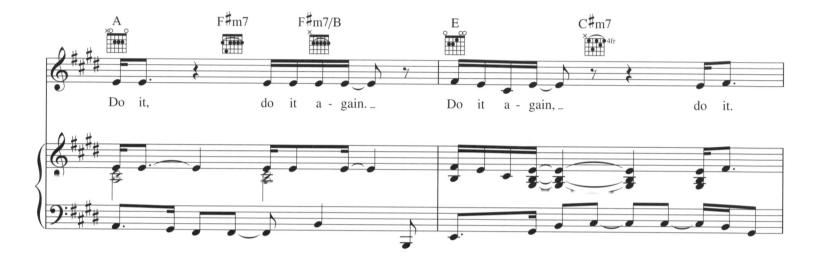

Do it, do it a - gain. _ Do it a - gain, _ do it.

Male: Now I like you, la - dy, so fine with your

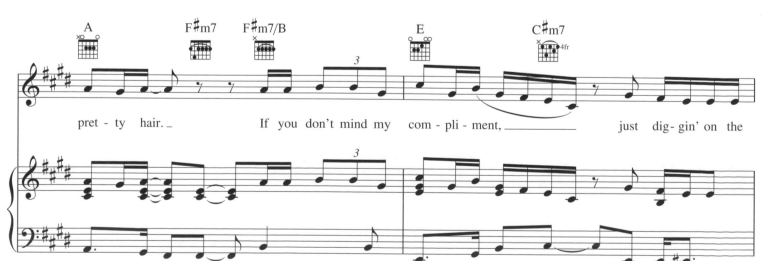

pret - ty hair. _ If you don't mind my com - pli - ment, _____ just dig - gin' on the

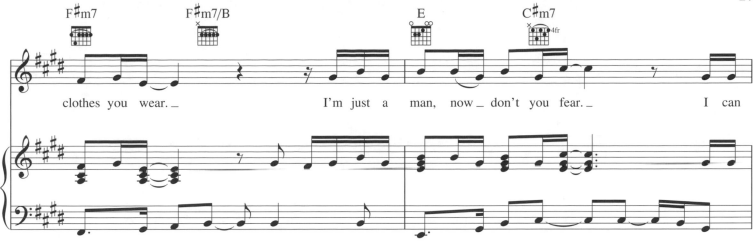

clothes you wear. _ I'm just a man, now _ don't you fear. _ I can

love you, now I brought you here. _ Wan-na do it a-gain, _ do it, uh, I wan-na do it a-gain. _

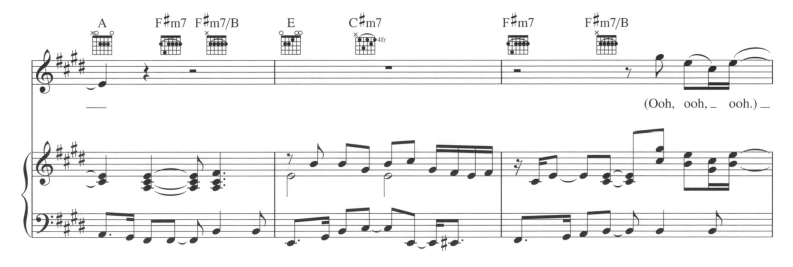

(Ooh, ooh, _ ooh.) _

Female: Like a ham-mer on the

block, love be-gan to rock. Give the sis-ter

love and pride, feel good and sat-is-fied. I'm not a

girl that could lin-ger, but I feel like a but-ter-fin-ger. I wan-na

D.S. al Coda

do it a-gain, do it a-gain, do it. Let's do it in the

I'LL TAKE YOU THERE

Words and Music by
ALVERTIS ISBELL

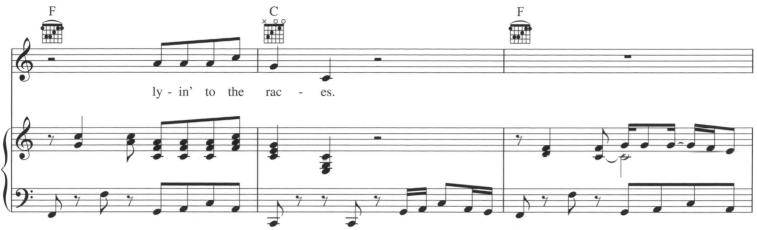

ly - in' to the rac - es.

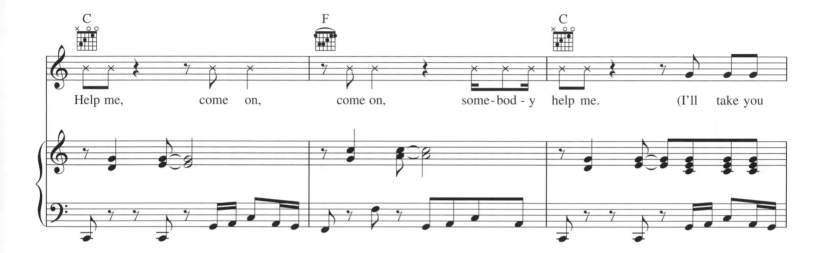

Help me, come on, come on, some - bod - y help me. (I'll take you

there.) Help me y'all. (I'll take you there.)

Help me now. (I'll take you there.) (I'll take you

there.)   Mer- cy, (I'll take you there.)

Let me take you there. (I'll take you there.)   Let me take you. (I'll take you

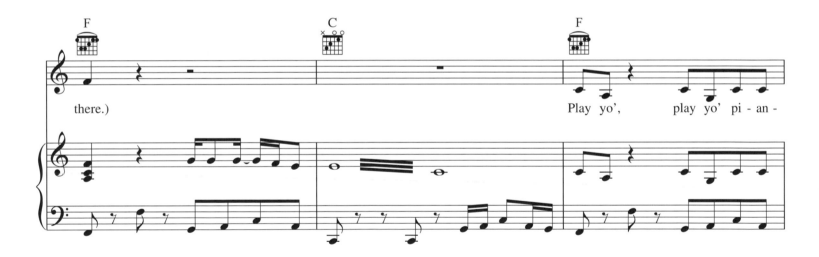

there.)   Play yo', play yo' pi - an -

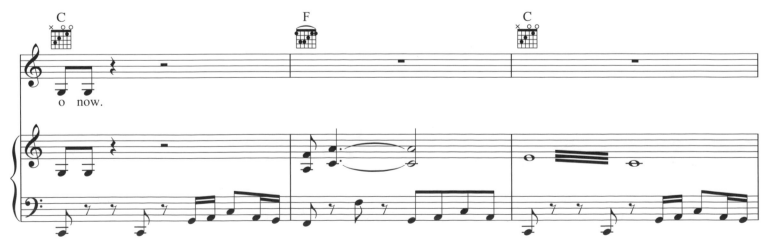

o now.

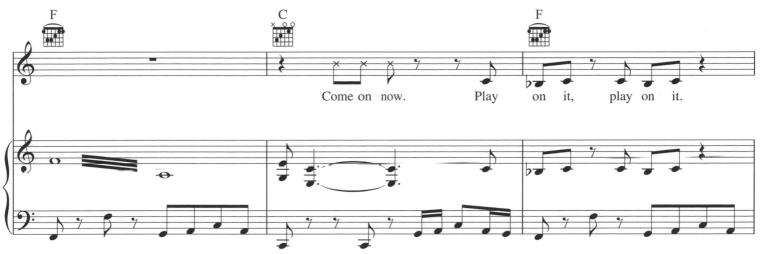

Come on now. Play on it, play on it.

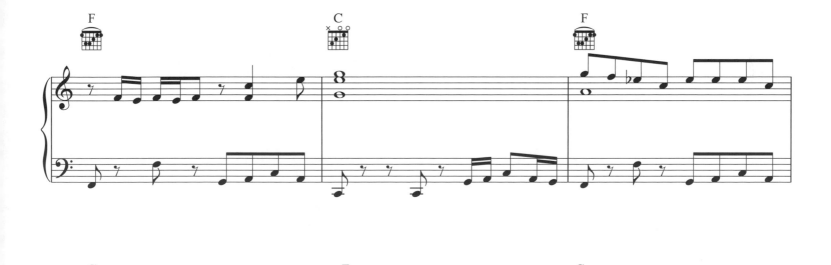

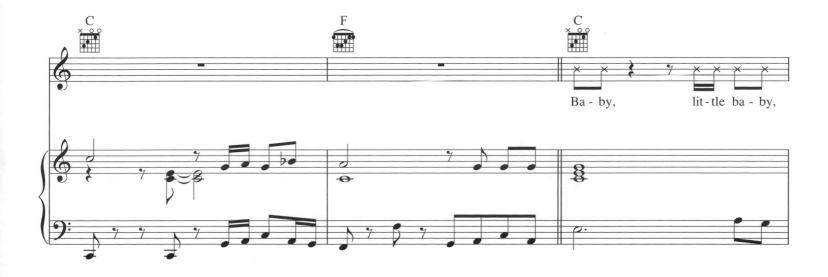

Ba- by, lit- tle ba- by,

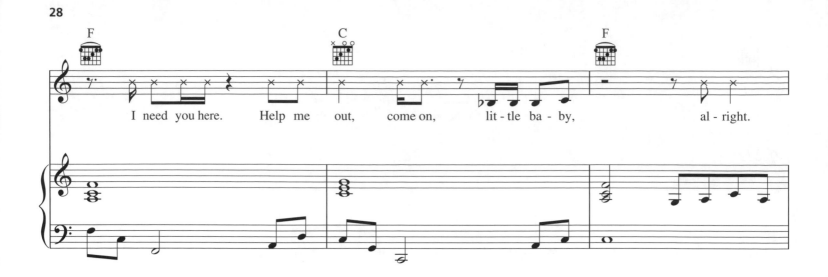

I need you here. Help me out, come on, lit - tle ba - by, al - right.

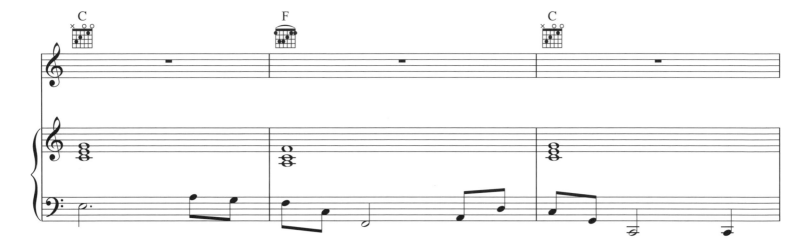

I, oh, I, I know a

place, y'all, (I'll take you there.) ain't no - bod - y cry - in', (I'll take you

there.) ain't no-bod-y wor-ried, (I'll take you there.) no smil-in'

fac - es, (I'll take you there.) ly - in' to the

rac - es. (I'll take you there.)

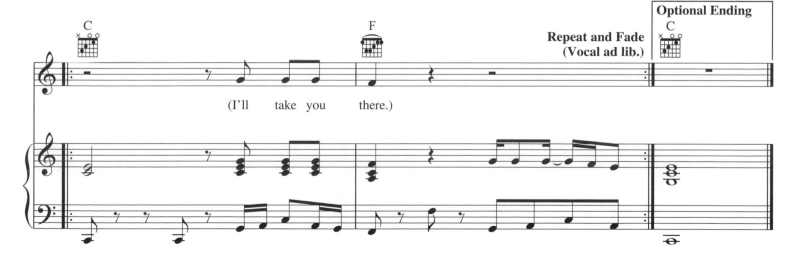

(I'll take you there.)

Repeat and Fade
(Vocal ad lib.)

Optional Ending

IF YOU'RE READY
(Come Go with Me)

Words and Music by HOMER BANKS,
CARL HAMPTON and RAYMOND JACKSON

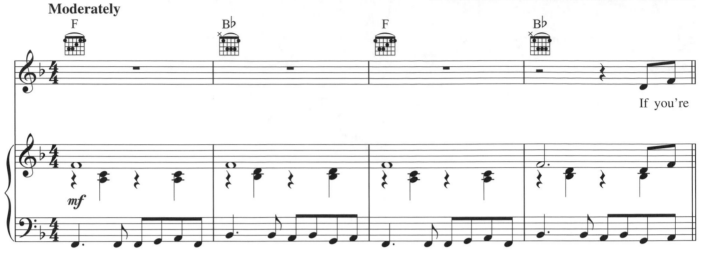

MY MAIN MAN
(He's My Main Man)

Words and Music by BETTYE JEAN CRUTCHER,
BOB MANUEL, LARRY NIX
and MACK RICE

Look o-ver my shoul-der now what do you think I see,
I've been a-round now a might-y long time,

me and my main man just him and me. 'Round the cor-ner now
I just dis-cov - ered he's a per-son-al friend of mine. Do you know how it feels

I found love me and my main man a-gainst the whole wide world.
to find some-thing real? Now that's my main man and that's the way I feel.

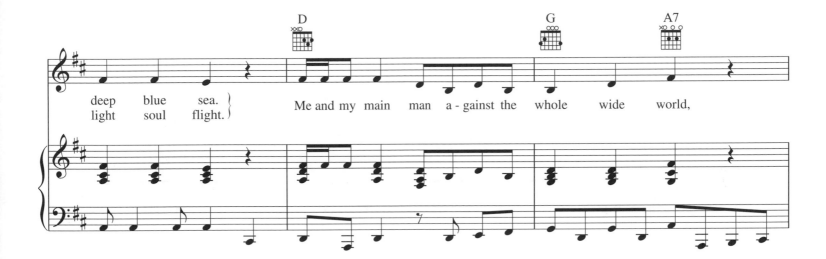

OH LA DE DA

Words and Music by
LEROY PHILLIP MITCHELL

Joyful Gospel-Rock

come on, _____ come on.) _____

And if you
And if you

(Come on, _____ come on, _____ come on.) _

feel like you wan - na sing, _____ come on, _____ hey, _ hey, _ hey.
want dis - crim - i - na - tion to end, _____ come on, _____ yeah. _____

Come on, _____ now,
Oh, oh, _____ oh,
ev - 'ry - bod - y sing a - long.

Ooh, _____ sing it now. Oh la de da.

Oh la de da. _____ Yeah,

C

oh la de da. _____ Yeah, oh la _____ de da.

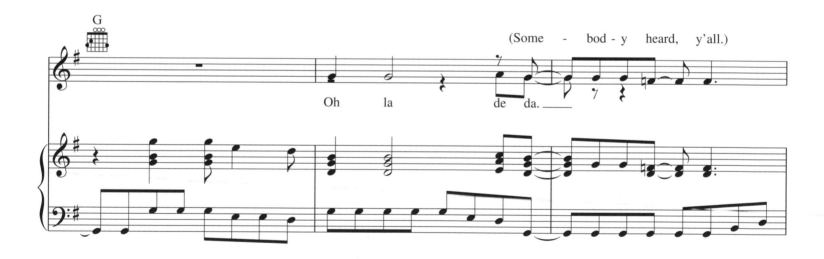

G

(Some - bod - y heard, y'all.)

Oh la de da. _____

Em   Am

Oh la de da. _____ Oh, oh, oh, _____ yeah, _____

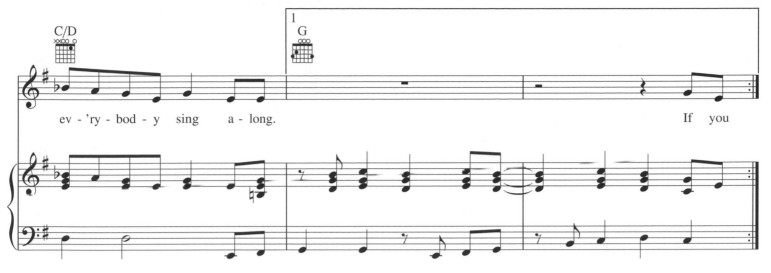

ev - 'ry - bod - y sing a - long. If you

If you

wan - na do your thing, do it now.
wan - na live in peace al - right.

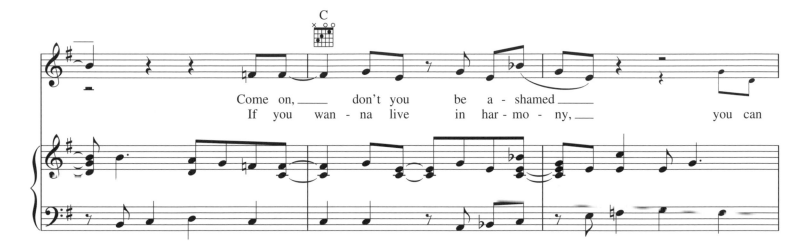

Come on, don't you be a - shamed
If you wan - na live in har - mo - ny, you can

(Oh la de da.)

do it. You can be a wom - an
Got to stand by

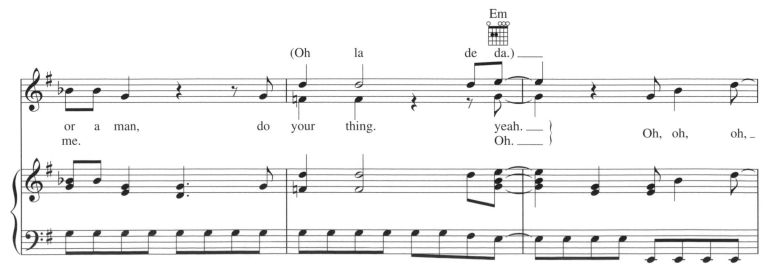

(Oh la de da.)

or a man, do your thing. yeah.
me. Oh. Oh, oh, oh,

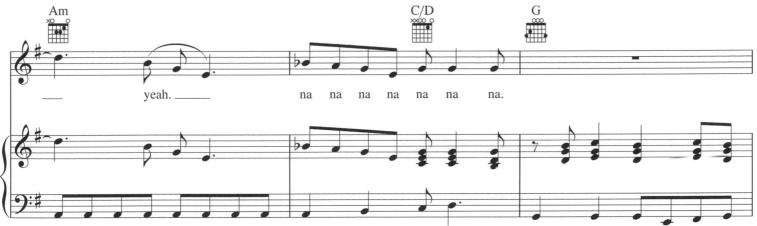

Oh la de da.

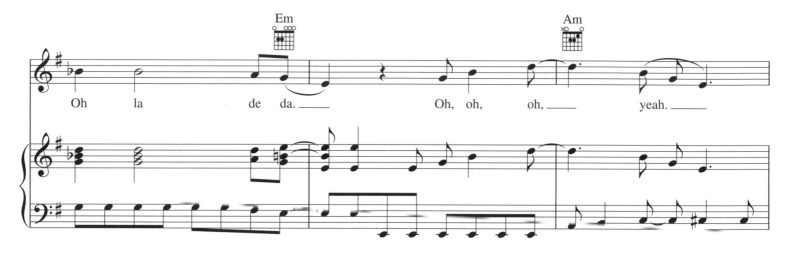

Oh la de da. _____ Oh, oh, oh, _____ yeah. _____

Repeat and Fade

na na na na na na na.

Optional Ending

na na na na na na na.

THIS WORLD

Words and Music by GARY FRIEDMAN
and HERB SHAPIRO

Bright Rock

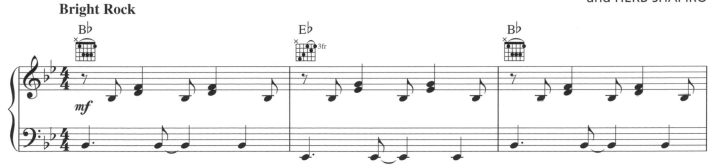

This world, this world, my

mind holds _ this world, my mind holds _ this

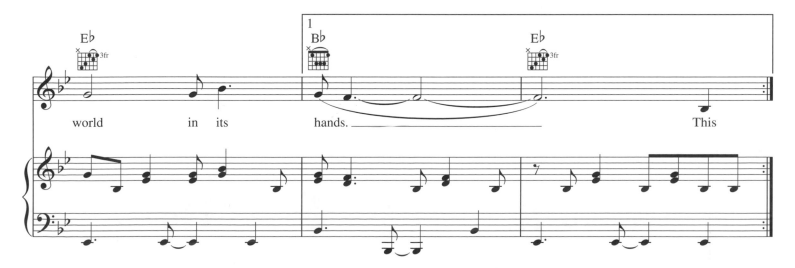

world in its hands. _____ This

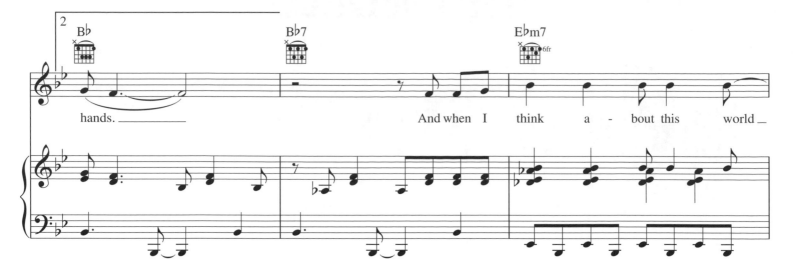

hands. _____ And when I think a - bout this world _

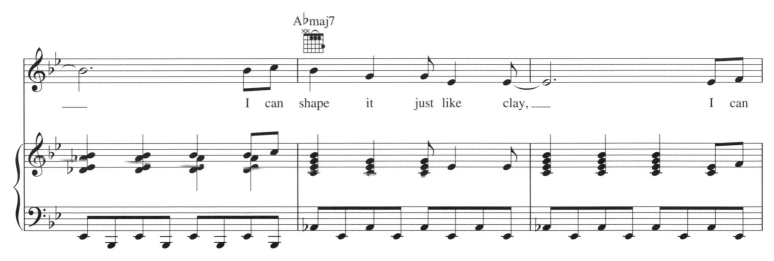

_ I can shape it just like clay, _ I can

make my - self _ a gar - den of E - den _ or

throw it all a - way _ This

world, this world, my mind holds _ this

world, my mind holds _ this world in its

hands. _____ This hands. _____

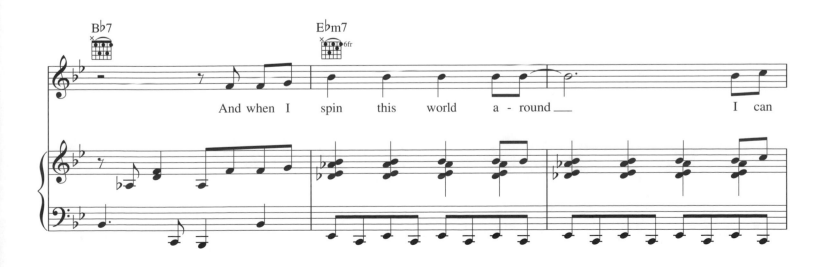

And when I spin this world a - round ___ I can

turn night in - to day, ___ I can make my - self a

sun - ny to - mor - row _____ or bring back yes - ter - day __

This world, this

world, my mind holds _ this world, my

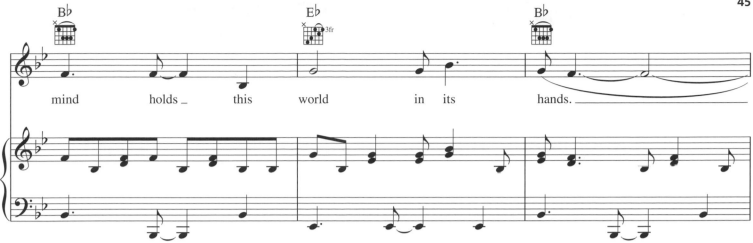

mind holds _ this world in its hands. _

_ This world, this world, my

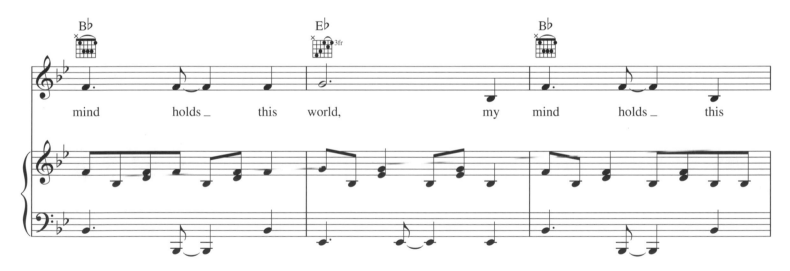

mind holds _ this world, my mind holds _ this

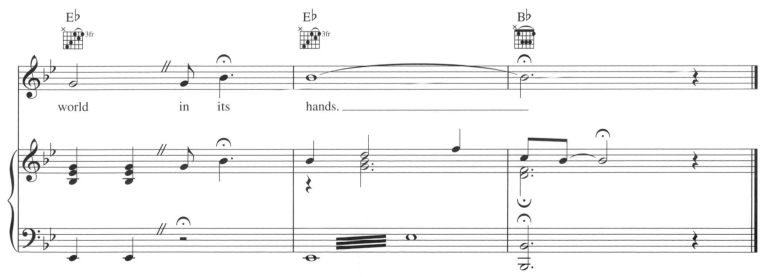

world in its hands. _

RESPECT YOURSELF

Words and Music by MACK RICE
and LUTHER INGRAM

sheet off your face, boy. It's a brand-new day.___
dumb e-nough to think it-'ll make___ you a big ol' man. }

Re-spect your-self.___ Re-spect your-self.___

Re-spect your-self.___ Re-spect your-self.___

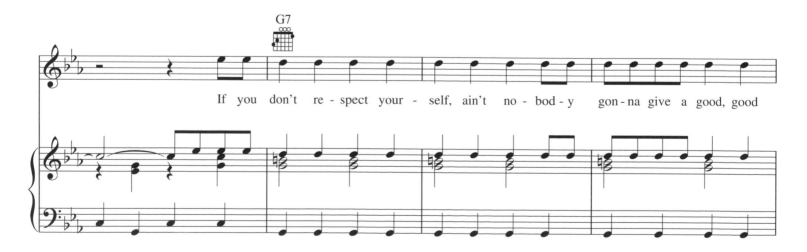

G7

If you don't re-spect your-self, ain't no-bod-y gon-na give a good, good

hoot! Re - spect your - self. ___ Re -

spect your - self. ___ Re - spect your - self. ___

Re - spect your - self. ___ If you're

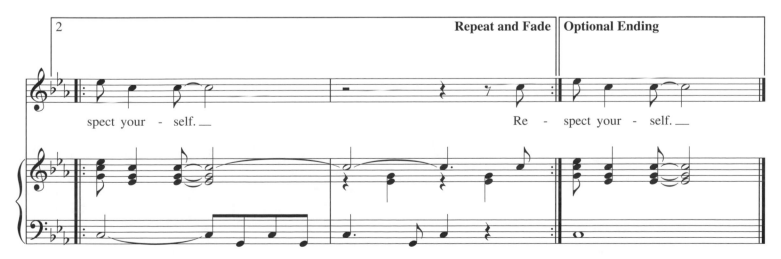

spect your - self. ___ Re - spect your - self. ___

YOU'VE GOT TO EARN IT

Words and Music by William "SMOKEY" ROBINSON
and CORNELIUS GRANT

Relaxed Soul Groove

To get stones __ from a rock, __ you've got to break it.
fire from match-es, you've got to strike 'em.
broke __ things work, __ you've got to fix 'em.

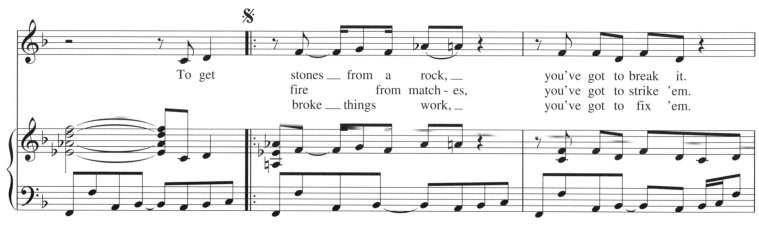

To get bread from dough, __
To get a feel-in' like this,
To make two things one, ___

you've got to bake it.
you've got to like it.
you've got to mix them.

To get
To get
To get

wa-ter from a fau-cet, you've got to turn it.
ash-es from_ wood, you've got to burn it.
but-ter from_ milk, you've got to churn it.
If you wan-na be loved,_

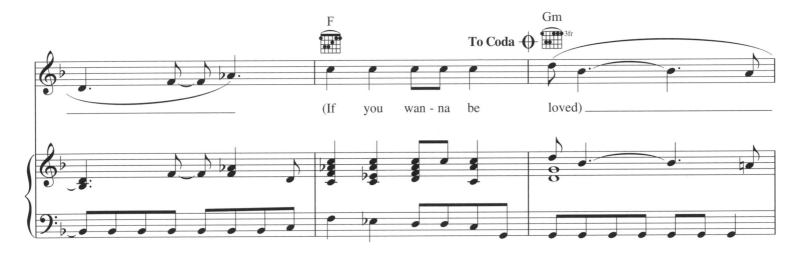

(If you wan-na be loved)_

you've got to earn it.

To get

Throw __ hate __ right out - ta your, _____

_____ your mind. *Flute and Trumpet Solos ad lib.*

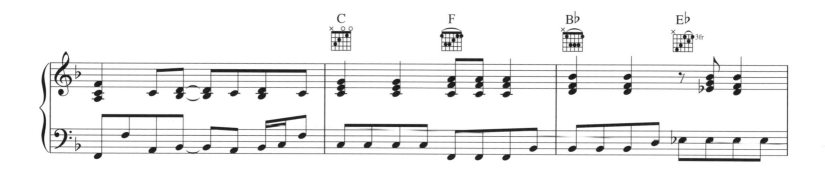

To make

D.S. al Coda

loved) _____ you got-ta earn it, earn it,

earn it. That's what you got-ta do, now. Earn ____ it.

Continue vocal ad lib. to end

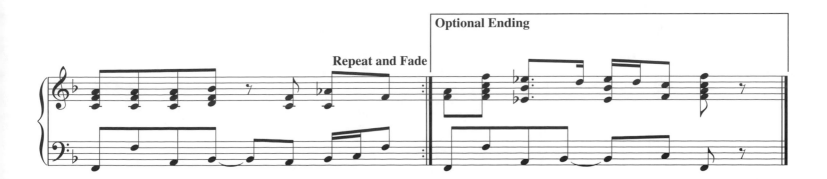

Repeat and Fade

Optional Ending

TOUCH A HAND, MAKE A FRIEND

Words and Music by CARL HAMPTON,
HOMER BANKS and RAYMOND JACKSON

Can't you feel it in your

bones?

you my friend? _ Ain't it time _ to come on in?

at - ti - tude _ of oth - er peo - ple _ just like you.

A change _ is com - in' on

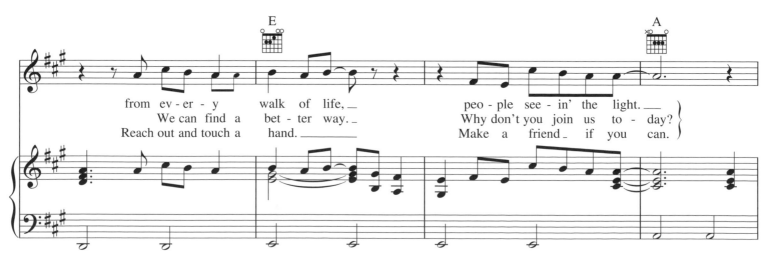

from ev - er - y walk of life, _ peo - ple see - in' the light. _

We can find a bet - ter way. _ Why don't you join us to - day?

Reach out and touch a hand. _ Make a friend _ if you can.

Can't you feel it in your heart now? __ A new thing is

tak - in' shape; reach out ___ and touch a hand,

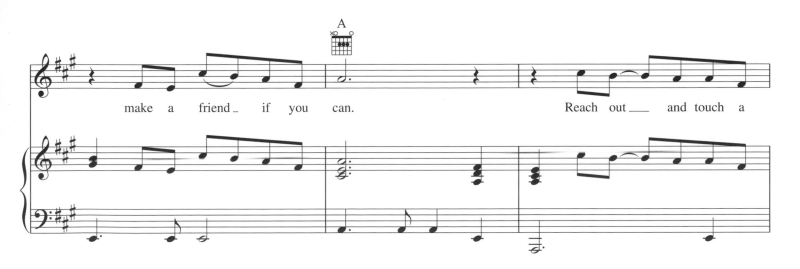

make a friend __ if you can. Reach out ___ and touch a

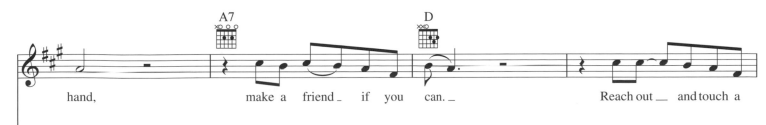

hand, make a friend __ if you can. __ Reach out __ and touch a